10001:
The Year of the Dog

The Memoirs of Snickers

10001: The Year of The Dog

The Memoirs of Snickers

ASSISTED BY HIS BELOVED FRIEND

Maurice Lind

Laurus Books

10001:
The Year of the Dog
The Memoirs of Snickers

ASSISTED BY HIS BELOVED FRIEND

Maurice Lind

Copyright © 2012 Maurice Lind

All rights reserved. No part of this book may be reproduced in any form without express written permission from the publisher, except in case of brief quotations in critical articles or reviews.

Paperback: ISBN-13: 978-0-9847683-6-3
E-Book: ISBN-13: 978-0-9847683-7-0

Edited and designed by Nancy E. Williams

Cover design by Jennifer Tipton Cappoen and Nancy E. Williams

ENDORSED BY  PUBLISHERS OF *Susie's Miracle*

PUBLISHED BY

LAURUS BOOKS
P. O. BOX 894
LOCUST GROVE, GA 30248 USA
WWW.THELAURUSCOMPANY.COM

PRINTED IN THE UNITED STATES OF AMERICA

This book may be purchased in paperback or eBook from TheLaurusCompany.com, Amazon.com, BarnesandNoble.com and other retailers around the world.

PARENTAL DISCRETION IS ADVISED:
Some parts of this book contain subject matter that may not be suitable for children.

Dedicated to
Snickers

Acknowledgements

I would like to express my sincere gratitude to the following people who were instrumental in this book becoming a reality:

Judy Turner, who did some of the initial editing and provided some good ideas for the organization of the text.

My wife, Sherry, who understood how many days, nights, and years it took to understand the thoughts of a dog. She loves Snickers as much as I do.

A special thanks to Nancy E. Williams of Laurus Books, who tried to understand Snickers and did the editing and layout to put the book into its final form.

Contents

Acknowledgements 6

10001: The Year of the Dog 9

The Laws of Dogs 17

Escape 23

Care Giving 31

Hiking 33

Begging 39

The Language of Dogs 47

The Way We Dogs Count 55

Famous Dogs 63

The Mayor's Race 67

Advice From Dogs To Humans 71

Sex & Reproduction 75

Bitches: Female Dogs 78

Our God 81

Dreams 83

10001 Revisited 91

Appendix 1 95

Appendix 2 97

10001: The Year of the Dog

According to ancient Chinese tradition, this was to be the year of the Ox, but we knew it would be the year of the DOG. We are not going to wait another nine years. We are ready now.

Some have stated that our ancestry was of wolves, some said it was of fish in the sea, some said, originally, of microbes in the boiling waters of early time. I like to think of its beginning (I mean our real evolutionary beginning) about the year 2000 AD with a very intelligent dog named SNICKERS. Yes, that is me. I am getting sleepy. Am I dreaming again? No, I think I am awake. No, maybe I am dreaming.

That is the year that our masters struggled with an overrated problem with ancient computers. They called it "Y2K" for "Year 2 Thousand." How could they know that in 8000 years, computer bugs would be immaterial to the

Sometimes I think I want to be a Husky and run in the Iditarod.

existence of masters. Notice that I did not say "our masters."

Allow me to enlighten you. First, sure, I am a dog. I am writing this book. Before you throw it in the garbage, please be a little patient with me. I am just a friendly dog.

My ancestors relayed tales to me that still make me very angry with humans. We have learned to control our anger, except for an occasional violent attack on a rebellious person. The stories usually started about how our forebearers often would be left to starve, or how our young would be killed in awful ways. We would be put into cages and left for days with little to eat or drink. We would be beaten with sticks and stones and left to die alongside of the roads where humans would drive machines that would run over us. Our bodies would lie for days until birds would finally carry us away where our souls could lie in peace.

Some of our masters were kind to us, and that is the only reason that we allowed the human race to survive. Well, we did have other motives and reasons that I shall talk about later. One of the stories that is still told over and over again follows. This is a happy story.

One of our cousin breeds was used in the North Country to pull sleds filled with humans and supplies. This breed is no longer a part of our domain since the breed evolved into another species. It took 5,000 years, but there was some gene tampering by humans, and the offspring of this species were

We all feel pain.

Dogs, Cats, and even Rhinos feel pain.

no longer *DOGS*. Anyway, before all of this happened, stories are that these "Huskies," as they were called, would do what humans made them do. They would run and run and run. It was what we were meant to do. We still do it when we have time.

Yet another story that is often told is of a breed that is also extinct, the Greyhound. Oh, what a dream. I am 8,000 years in the future. Greyhounds loved to run also. It was a wonderful sport for humans to bet on them and see how fast they could run. Funny how humans thought they controlled the greyhounds.

In the later years, before extinction, we are told that all of the greyhounds would get together each morning and plan the race. This went on for about fifty years. They were about ready to "cash in" on their newly-found game but still lacked communication skills with humans. Then one day a very smart hacker (dog language—*arf*, with a long Λ) broke the greyhound language code and found out what the greyhounds had been doing.

The following years were cruel and terrible for all racing dogs. Most were killed. The few that escaped were lost into the gene pool of wild dogs, and therefore, the breed disappeared. But, while they lived, they ran and ran and ran. Oh, we know now that death ends a life but it doesn't end a relationship. We still remember the greyhounds, and if there is a dog heaven (no, we don't know that yet), they are still

In my next life, I want to be able to run as fast as a gazelle, so I can win a Greyhound Race with the big dogs.

running to see who can win the race.

I could go on and on about why we worked so long and hard to overcome humans. We have tried to forgive and forget, but we still have some in our population who are rebels. I will go into much detail later explaining the procedures and skills we used to overcome the human race, but let me say at this point that it was rather easy, as the human race became greedier and greedier. They (humans) really allowed all of this to happen. We, the DOGS, were at the right place at the right time to capitalize on it.

Wake up. Wake up. You can go back to sleep later. It is time for lunch.

I don't want lunch now. I want to dream some more.

How many Laws, or Commandments, do dogs have? Read on …

The Laws of Dogs

1. Any dog that intentionally breaks a law shall be killed by the pack immediately.

2. A dog must share his food with young puppies or with old dogs over 1,023 years old—75 in human years. Our method of counting will be explained in a later chapter. The actual time is really related to our gestation period along with several other variables.

3. A dog cannot dominate any other species, except humans, gorillas, and cats. A bit of explanation is due here. Humans … obvious. Gorillas … they have nearly acquired the intelligence necessary to overcome us. We must protect against that. Cats … we never could stand them and never will let them have any freedom.

10. Dogs may mate forever if they so choose. That is fine, but no divorce and no cheating. If caught cheating, a dog

must die. Remember, all laws must be followed. A dog does not have to mate for life. This gives him or her free reign to all dogs that are not mated for life. The exceptions are dogs under the age of 12 (6) dog years or over the age of 1,002 dog years *(I am not going to convert for you any more)*. These young dogs and old dogs are protected. If this law is broken, then there will be death to the intruder. You question how we can tell how old we are? We can tell by our teeth and voice tone.

11. Dogs never have to share their house and pen with anyone who is not in the age defined in law #2. They must share with the old and the young, if needed. Our reason is that all dogs of working age must work and find a home and support their families. You question, "How about sick dogs?" We don't let them be sick over two days. If they are not well in two days, then we, the pack, kill them. We have no doctors, no hospitals, no medicine except natural, and no sick dogs.

12. Any dog may live as long as he is not sick. Some of us live a long time and become very wise, but if we exhibit sickness for two days, law #11 takes over. This gives us great peace. We know that we will never suffer long.

13. Dogs must never invade another dog's territory except

The Laws of Dogs

for the following reasons:

A. To mate with free dogs.

B. To discuss new boundary lines.

C. To conduct our business. I mean bathroom business. You see, that is the only way we can expand our territory. Plus, we think it is FUNNY.

20. A dog must never fight unless he catches someone using "Exception C" above. Then he can do whatever is necessary to chase the intruding dog away, but be aware that if injured in the fight, either dog might be put to death by the pack.

21. Dogs will gain rank over other dogs only by intelligence. All dogs must take all tests every ten years to determine the ranking of the pack. The top three dogs will have to participate in endurance tests to determine the ranking of the top three dogs. The endurance testing will consist of running, jumping, and ladder climbing.

22. A ranked dog is the only dog that does not have to dig bones. All other dogs must dig at least one hole per day and must bury food every other day. This is the only law for which a death penalty does not exist. If the law is broken, the dog must go hungry for twelve days, and

then he will be reinstated into the pack.

23 Any dog, male or female, that contributes to having more than three puppies each twelve years will be sterilized for life. We have very few dogs that break this law anymore. We have a very stable population in relation to our food supply.

30. A dog may have only one human master. We still call them "masters" even though we are in control and are the real masters. Those dogs without masters must wait until they are above the mean level of intelligence as determined by law #21, until they can apply for a master. Masters are assigned by bone lottery. Some day we hope to breed enough humans so all of us can have masters. For some unknown reason, humans continue to kill each other for what we think are silly reasons, like money, land, religion, mates, etc. No wonder we were able to master them.

31. No dog shall ever acquire more possessions than the total possessions of any other two dogs in the pack. If that occurs, their possessions are distributed equally among the pack.

Wake up! Wake up! You are in my bed! Go do your counting exercises!

Escape

There are many ways that we use to escape. We learned this during the time when our masters dominated us.

The first and foremost way was to dig under whatever enclosure we were in at the time. Sometimes it was a fence made out of lattice, sometimes wire, sometimes brick, often just plain wood.

The material didn't matter. What mattered was whether we could dig under the fence. We were born and bred to dig. We have sharp claws to dig and dig and dig. Many times, the front feet get going so fast that we forget to use our back feet to push away all the excess dirt. The only problem is that sometimes we hit a tree root or some other obstacle that just will not come out. Then we have to employ another tool.

That is when our sharp teeth come into play. Get all the dirt out of the way and then grab the root with your teeth and

pull and pull and pull. Most of the time, this technique does not work. Brawn without brains is useless. Try chewing on that root. Sometimes it tastes terrible. If it is a small root, chew one end off, move over about eight to ten inches, more if you are a big dog. Chew it again, and pull the piece out with your teeth. Success. Now, dig some more until you can get your whole body under the fence. Be especially careful that you don't try to wedge your body under the fence until the hole is big enough. Nothing is worse than getting your head and part of your body through and then getting stuck. All you can do then is bark to let your master know where you are. Then you will be punished, and the fence will be secured better with stakes that cannot be dug around.

If your fence is built on concrete, forget about digging under it. That situation requires a second alternative.

Can you jump over the fence? Some of us were born with long and strong legs. If you are a short-legged dog, forget this technique. Get a running start. Six to eight feet is fine. Then give a strong push with your back legs, jumping up and over. Didn't quite make it? Try it again. This time, go about half way and get a good foothold with your back feet about half way to the top. Give another big push with your back legs while pulling with your front legs and over you will go. But wait. I forgot to tell you to make sure you know what is on the other side of the fence. It could be a bottomless pit

I am out of here!

filled with alligators. It could be a pile of cow manure. It could be an ancient torture machine for bad dogs. It could be almost anything that you can imagine. Just be sure that you know.

Are there any other choices for escape other than under or over the fence? Through the fence might work. Sometimes the fence is made out of flimsy wood. Grab a piece of it in your mouth and pull and chew and jump up and down and chew some more, and finally, it starts to tear or break. Pretty soon, you have a hole big enough to crawl through. Make sure you look through the hole before you go through to see what is on the other side. And remember, no matter how you escape, there is always the chance that you won't like the outside. So make sure your return route is well planned.

Now, this is the best plan of escape. In fact, they nicknamed me "Houdini" because I used this method so often. Make a lot of racket. Bark and bark and bark until your master comes to see what is wrong. When he opens the gate and bends down to put on your leash, make a quick getaway between his legs, and you are free for a little while. This method doesn't work more than once or twice, so you have to rely on a variety of escape techniques to keep everyone confused.

You must realize that there is usually punishment for escaping. When you return from your adventure outside your pen, try one of these ruses. Come up to your master panting with saliva running out of your mouth like you are dying of thirst. They will run and get you some water. Gulp it down, and start licking them, and all will be forgotten. Another good idea is to fake an injury. Limp with one back leg. Don't overdo it, or they might take you to the Vet. That is a no-no. My favorite ruse is to look real ashamed and mournful. They will feel sorry for you and might even go into the house and bring you out a treat. That is killing two birds with one stone. You escaped, you had fun running in the neighborhood, and you got a reward for it.

Some dogs are not put into a pen but are contained by cruel methods. Well, I think they are cruel anyway. Well, maybe not cruel but just rather confining. I must admit, some dogs even like these methods. Some are crate trained. How do you escape from a crate? It takes a little planning ahead of time. When you know that you are about to be put into your crate, pick up a small stick in your mouth. When they are about to close the latch, push the stick into the latch so that it doesn't close properly. Now, when your boss has gone, push and pull on the little gate, and it will open. You are free.

Some dogs are tied to a long line with a leash. The only way to escape this containment is to chew the leash into two pieces. You will get punished for this, so make sure the escape is worth the later punishment.

Okay. I am awake now. I must go back to real life.

Now here is a true life experience of what can happen when you escape too often. I have two homes. I have one home in one state and another in another state. Let us call them home A and home B. I have a daytime deck that is nearly impossible to get out of unless you are a good jumper and can jump over the three-foot enclosure around the deck. I have never escaped from this deck.

I live during the summer months in home B. My master had returned to home A for a few days and was told by the police and the neighbors that his dog was running loose and needed to be caught and put in a safe enclosure, or he would be captured and placed in a dog pound. They said they had repeatedly caught me and put me on the deck, and the next day I would be gone to roam the streets again. All the while, I was a thousand miles away at my summer home. They had been putting the wrong dog into my abode, and of course, he would just jump over the railing and head for his real home.

My master, not wanting a dog that had a police record, called the local authorities and explained that I was not the loose dog, and would they please remove my name from the wanted list.

Be careful. Who knows what lurks beyond closed gates?

At peace with the world.

Care Giving

My master and I walked into the room. Well, let me restate that. My master's wife and I walked into the room. We were at an extended care facility, and we had returned for our second year of visiting the patients. I loved the work. Would Mr. Henderson remember me? Last year, he would always let me jump onto his bed. He would scratch my ears, and I would lick his face. I know that I brought great joy to all the patients.

We walked into the first room. There is Mr. Henderson. He looked at us. "I know that you are Snickers, but who is that person with you?" So sad for my master's wife, for she had given so much of her time so that I could visit with the patients. Yes, they remembered me, and today, I brought joy to some very old people. I am sure I must have reminded them of one of their dogs from their childhood. It is so wonderful to give enjoyment to someone else.

Today, I will lead all of the hikers to worlds unknown.

Hiking

I started hiking with humans when I was just a young pup. I knew that eventually I would be the leader of the entire hiking group. There was a big, brown lab who was currently in that position. I was allowed to be second in line. I was a good friend with the leader, but I am an Alpha dog, so I just waited.

Unfortunately, the leader became sick and had to be put to sleep. I really miss her, but I was moved into her position.

My masters would get a phone call on Sunday mornings, and I would recognize the man's voice. I knew today would be a great hike. I couldn't contain the excitement. I would jump up and down, bark, and pester my masters to hurry. It was time to go.

I love to get on the trail. There are those great smells, odors as you call them, at every turn. If they would just let me off my leash, I would catch that tiger. Well, maybe it is

It is a steep mountain, but I know I can make it to the top.

just a chipmunk, but I would pretend that it is a tiger.

Today, we go to a nice lake with a trail the entire way around it. There are a lot of humans and also a lot of dogs. When we get to the starting point, I have to say hello to everyone in the hiking group. They all know me and pet me and rub my ears. Oh, it is so good to be known and loved. My ego is inflated today. I am the leader of the group. Every time I meet another dog, we need to do dog things, of course.

I love all dogs, but every now and then I meet a dog that is a bit unfriendly and will try to snip at me. "Don't mess with me, boy. I am in charge today." We hike around the lake a couple of times and then go onto some other trails.

There is one place that I must tell you about. It is a small pond where fish are raised. There is a brick wall around it, but I can jump up on it. When I was a little puppy, my masters would carry me around it, but now I have learned that I can run the whole way around the pond on the brick wall. My masters tell me that it is one foot wide. Remember, we dogs have little feet, so to us it is about six feet wide. My master takes off my leash and tells me to "go." I jump up on the wall and run as fast as I can. Sometimes, I get going too fast and miss a turn, fall off, take a real tumble, jump back up again, and run to the finish point. A group of humans are always there to congratulate me on my good trick.

One day a couple of years ago, we decided to hike part

of the Appalachian Trail. The hike was to be about 13 miles in human terms. Remember, the number 13 is really 31 (refer to appendix) in dog numbers. The trail was at a very high altitude. My master took me off my leash so that I could run as fast as I wanted to go. I was the leader. I would run to the front of the group, but then I would run back to see how my master was doing. He wasn't doing too well. He was getting farther and farther behind. Now and then, he would put my leash back on, and I would pull him for a while to get him to hurry up. I ran back to the front. They don't know where to go without me. Back to my master, back to the front. I am traveling many more miles than I had expected. I was going to be the hero of the day. It was getting dark, and we still had three miles to go. Some of the group was getting worried that we would have to spend the night on the mountain. I would protect them from the lions and the tigers and woodchucks and chipmunks.

It was nearly dark, and we had to go down a very rocky path to the end. I can do it. I have 10 (4) legs. But these old ladies will fall. I can't let that happen. I bark and bark, and soon a man comes on an ATV. He says, "I will lead you down a different trail with the lights on my vehicle." I run in front. I am the hero of the day. After about an hour, we reach the end. I will live in infamy for getting everyone to safety. When I finally returned home that evening, I crawled into my house and slept for eight hours without waking.

My masters still talk about that day. Unfortunately, they forget who was the leader. Oh, well. I still tell the story to my friends around the campfire. Then there was the time that I was in the middle of Africa ... uh-oh, you won't believe that one.

Proper begging
is an art form.

Begging

This is an art form. Did you hear me? Begging is a form of art in the canine world. It came about by way of many years of evolution, as I mention elsewhere, but it is so important that we must devote an entire chapter to the subject. If you do not beg, you do not live with quality. Allow me to state it in a different way. If you do not beg, you do not live a life of getting treats that usually are for humans only.

First, the forbidden rules, which you must remember. Never beg at a formal dinner party. That will get you sent outside immediately with no rewards and a scolding by your master saying something like, "Dogs in this house know better than to beg." This is what he tells his guests anyway. Little do they know that we always beg for something to eat. Never beg and drool at the same time. Keep your mouth shut until that Pavlov response goes away. If there is more than

Wrong environment for begging.

one dog in your household, don't compete with the other dog. Let him do the begging. When the morsel is thrown to him, bump him a little so that he misses the toss, and beat him to the snack. Never go from one person to the other begging. You will only start a feud between the persons at the table as to which one of them you like best. You will end up with nothing, everyone will start arguing about many different subjects, and you will be banished to the outside, being blamed for all the commotion.

The rules for proper begging follow. You are the beggar, the human is the beggee. Start the beg. Meanwhile, sit very patiently, looking hungry and mournful. Don't sit up with your front feet in the air yet. Stare directly at the beggee. If he or she looks away, give a slight whimper to get his attention again. Be sure not to overdo this voice effect. At the right time, rise up, with your front feet in the air. Smile just a little bit. No one can resist that look. That little piece of pork chop is about to come your way. Be ready. If you catch it, you will be praised, and you are one step closer to becoming a seasoned beggar. If you miss it, go fetch and try to start the game of catch and miss and go fetch, catch and miss and go fetch. That technique might get you five or six pieces of pork chop. When you finally learn to catch 99% of the throws, you are on your way to becoming an exhibitor at every meal.

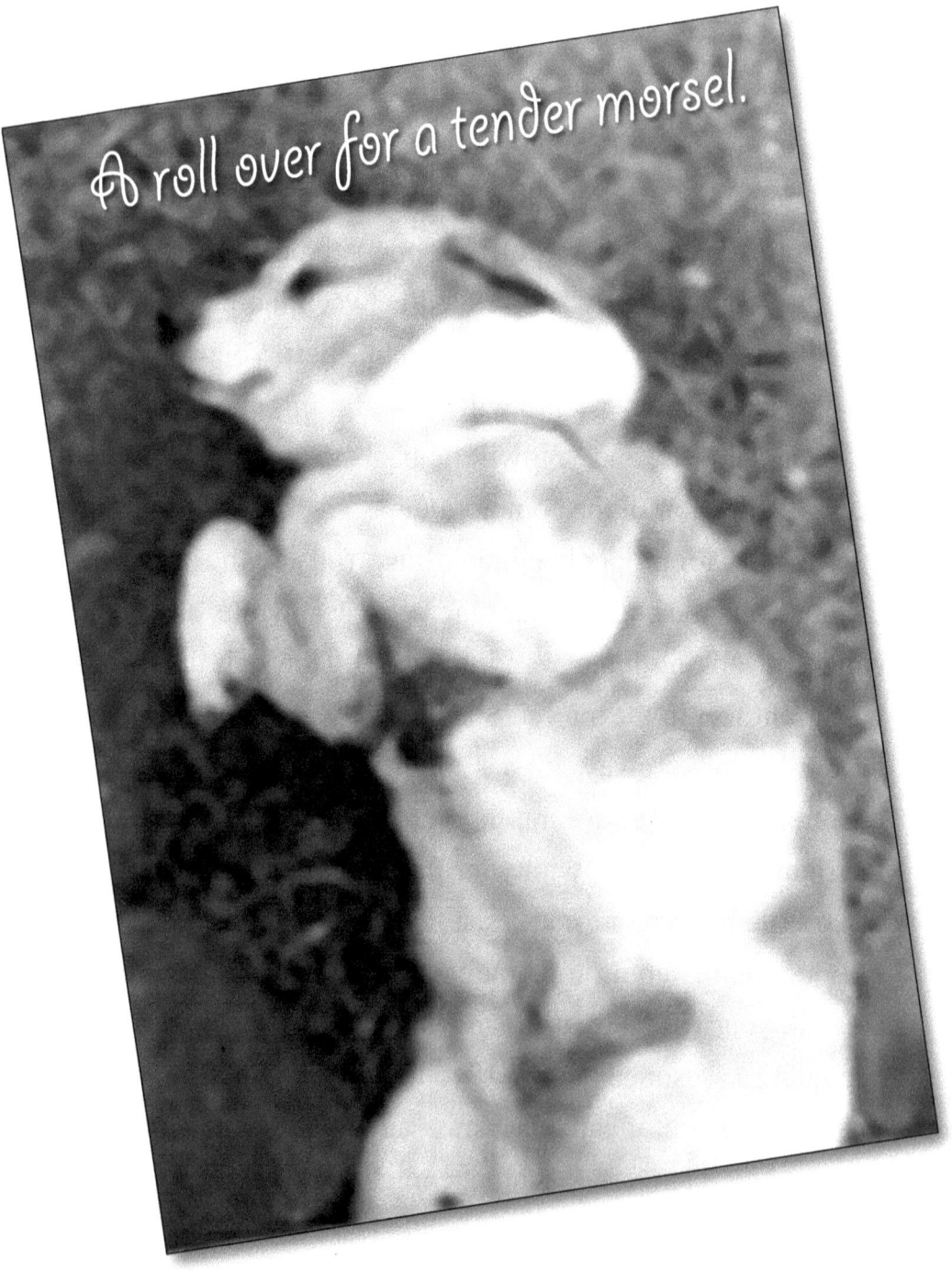
A roll over for a tender morsel.

Sometimes the above method just does not work. Your master is one of those persons who does not recognize the physical and psychological needs of canines. You must first get his attention.

If you are outside and the door is closed, you might as well forget it. Let us assume that you are inside, and you are ready to start the training of your master. Within sight of your master, do a couple of rollovers. If he doesn't respond, do a few more. Still no recognition, do a flip. Make sure you have practiced this in private so that you can do it perfectly. If he doesn't see you, give a little yip and do it again. Someone at the table will say, "Isn't he cute? Where did he learn that? Give him a reward." You are winning. Roll over = a piece of cookie. Flip = a piece of steak. Roll over and a flip combination = a whole sweet biscuit.

Now, I will tell you the best of all table techniques. It is not called "begging." It is just getting treats without anyone knowing about it. This usually works best when there are young children at the table. Listen to the conversation and when you hear something like, "Sally, eat those ???????? on your plate," nudge Sally's leg a little to show her that you are around, and she will carefully hand you those ??????? from her plate that she doesn't want to eat. I have even trained some older people to feed me their broccoli and brussels sprouts that they didn't want. Don't ever reveal your

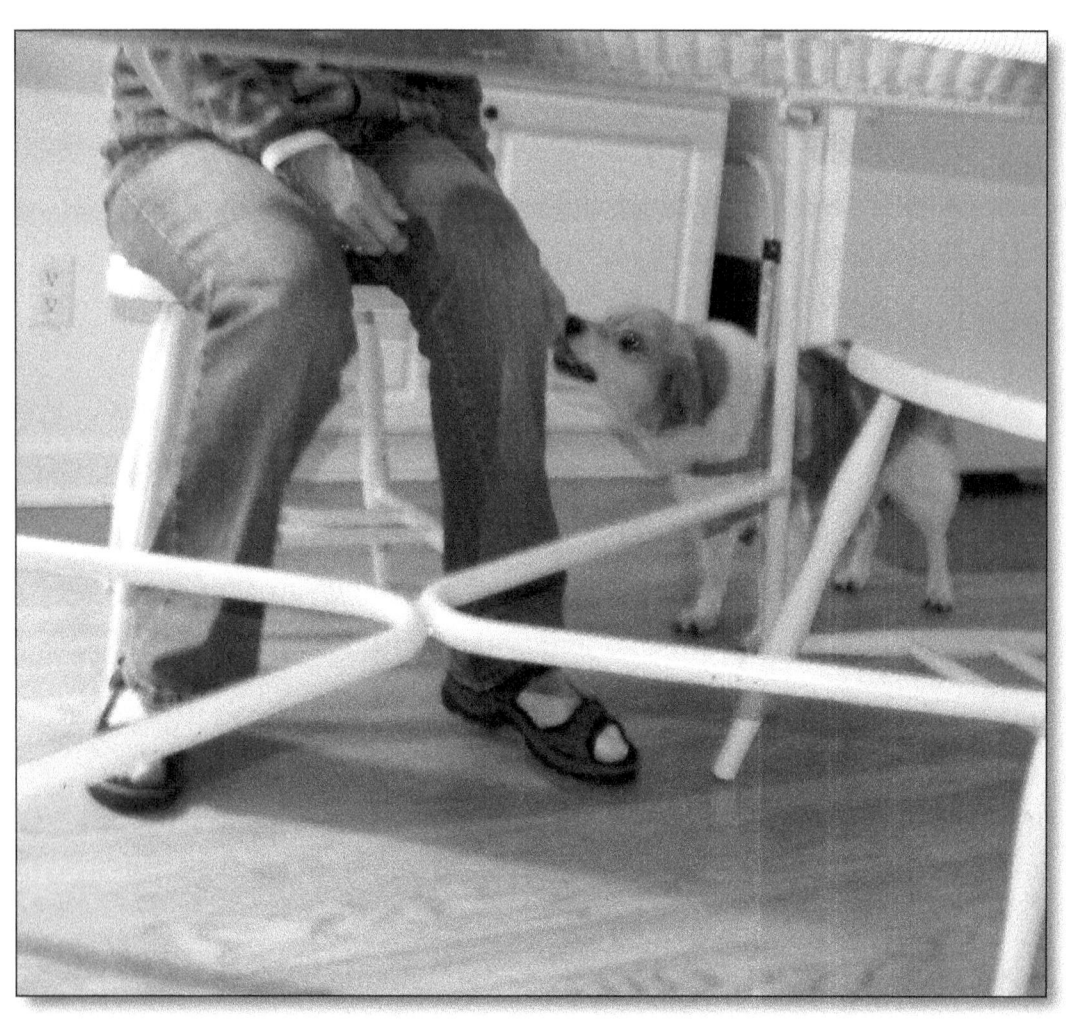

"Don't tell anyone, and
I will eat all of your carrots
that you do not want."

strategy. The kids will never tell. Every child I know has, at one time or the other, used a friendly dog to help them clean their plate, and everyone is happy, especially we canines.

Oh, I am so full, and there is a nice blanket. I think I will take a little nap. Perhaps I can dream of 10001 again.

Ever onward I must go.

My name is Orillagagonny.

The Language of Dogs

There was always a theory among humans that language was necessary for reasoning. The reverse might also be debated. This dilemma was not resolved. Let me discuss the dog's view of it. Oh, boy, I am going into one of my vivid dreams again.

It seems that over the years, certain primates had developed the ability to vocalize certain sounds in their imitation of human speech. They adopted what people in the 20th century called a "Pig Latin" type of language. I personally think that this name was a slam at the intelligence of the pig, but so be it. Anyway, the primates' language, especially the gorilla's, was called "rumbagonny" language. Now, as we look back on it, it was sort of juvenile, but let me give you an example: "Come over tonight" would sound like "OMECAGONNY VEROERONNY ONIGHTTERONNY."

If they were especially romantic that night, she would

We all feel pain.

reply: "JIAGONNY MAAGONNY SAAGONNY OTHAGONNY SAAGONNY BAAGONNY ISTOLPERONNY." It took a long time for humans, us dogs, and all other animals to understand them, but we soon realized that their grunts and groans all followed a pattern.

The humans tried to fit their language into the gorilla's grunts, and vice versa. Humans were, excuse me, so stupid about their outlook on all things, i.e., everything had to be humanized. God was created in human form, not man in God's form. Language had to be in human form, not in animal form. Emotion had to be as humans experienced it, not as animals experienced it.

Pain was expressed as humans felt it. They never realized that a raccoon dead or dying on the road also felt pain and longed to be at home with his children and family. Life was short for some species, but it was still life for them.

If I seem a bit bitter, it is because we dogs hope to never make the mistake of thinking that the only important species is the DOG.

Let us go back to language again. We would get so tired of the words "sit," "stay," "roll over," "bad dog," "good dog," etc., etc. Hey, if you had told us just once in our language, we would have understood it immediately. We heard the word "sit" so much at first that we thought that was our name. What is this thing "Rover"? I thought my name

Who am I?

Good dog. Bad dog.

Good dog. Bad dog.

Bad dog. Good dog.

was "Sit." Why did you call the neighbor dog, "Shut up, you bitch"? I always called her "Sophie."

What about this idea that you can't reason without a language? We dogs do not use a human-like language. How do you think we obtained all the bones that we buried for leaner days? Oh, of course, you said it was instinct that forced us to bury our over-supply. Let me tell you, we would ponder whether to have a feast tonight or store up the bones for a rainy day. We never forgot where they were, and if a stray dog came around, we made sure he knew that this was *our* investment in the future.

We dogs still have a bit of a problem believing that cats can reason. Our elders who have more wisdom than we have keep telling us that it is our bias that makes us believe as we do. We certainly do not want to make the same mistake that humans did in believing that only their species had certain powers but, after all, *those damn black cats…*

There was a time in the distant past, as recorded by our former human masters, that intelligence was being created by machines. They called it "artificial intelligence." These machines were very powerful, and fast. They could try billions of approaches to problems. They remembered which approaches did not work and, therefore, never made the same mistake a second time. That is a true heuristic approach to problem solving. This technique was very popular for many

It is morning. I must wake up.
I must wake up.

years. Unfortunately, it was one of the symptoms of the faltering of the human race. If you turn over your life to a machine, it will soon dominate you ...

We dogs realize this mistake that humans made. We realize that artificial intelligence is only useful if you have set criteria that determines a right solution from a wrong solution. What did you humans call it, *a set of mores*? We have our rules as stated elsewhere. It is easy for us to solve problems. Besides, we don't have attorneys or courts or prisons. We want to live and be happy. The decision is right if it benefits our society. It is wrong if it destroys our society. We don't need a machine to decide that for us.

Wake up! That is the sun rising in the East. Wake up. It is still a long time until the year 10001.

Okay, I am awake now.

Ten toes look funny!

The Way We Dogs Count

I am learning how to count.

0, 1, 2, 3

My master is always leaving me for a few days, and he tells me, "I'll be back in five days."

Wait. Wait. Wait.

Or he says, "I will be back in two weeks."

0, 1, 2. How long is two weeks?

Or he says "I will be back in three hours."

Oh, boy, I get to eat in three hours.

Well, let me tell you, I just had to learn how to count. My only problem is, I do not have ten fingers and ten toes. I have four paws. I do have things that look like toes, but I didn't think to use them.

Maybe … maybe, I need to think for a while.

Let me see. I know that 0 (zero) means no "paws."

I know that 1 (one) means 1 "PAW."

I know that 2 (two) means 2 "PAWS."

My master said ten bones.

What does that mean?

How many pieces?

I know that 3 (three) means 3 "PAWS."

I understand "ALL PAWS" = AP.

I understand "ALL PAWS" + 1. AP + 1

I understand "ALL PAWS" + 2. AP + 2

I understand "ALL PAWS" + 3. AP + 3

Every time that I try to lift all my paws, I fall on my butt.

I understand the concept of lifting all my paws though (that's a big word).

If you said, "ten bones," it meant all my paws 2 times + 2.

If you said, "I have fifteen pieces of food for you," it meant, all my paws 3 times + 3. We are going to call that AP + AP + AP + 3.

My master uses a funny symbol 15 for this number.

How many pieces of food in the bowl?

I don't know yet.

My master said, "I will be back in twenty-five days." What does that mean? I waited and waited. Twenty-five, twenty-five days. I just lay on my blanket and waited and waited.

One day, my neighbor dog happened to come by. I call him Dumb Dog because he never has learned to count. But maybe he could help me. After all, he does have four paws.

Dumb Dog = DD.

Please refer to Appendix 1.

Remember: ALL PAWS = AP = 10.

To you humans, AP = 4.

AP + 1 = 11

AP + 2 = 12

AP + 3 = 13

And 2 AP + 3 = 23, etc.

To you humans, this is your number 11.

I am trying to help you.

"Thanks, Snickers."

𝒟𝓊𝓂𝒷 𝒟𝑜𝑔 = 𝒟𝒟

This is what happened. I thought if I continue counting 0, 1, 2, 3, ALL PAWS, ALL PAWS +1, ALL PAWS +2, ALL PAWS +3, and on and on and on …

About this time, Dumb Dog (DD) lifts his leg to go to the bathroom.

Eureka! (Now what does that mean?) Eureka! Eureka! I barked, and I barked. I have found it. I have found it!

"Dumb Dog, hold that position for a while." Dumb Dog did what he was told. So there he was with one paw in the air, which meant three paws were on the ground. I was thinking to myself, "Three times all my paws + 3." I realized that he could represent my next position in my number. My next number is DD + zero + zero. I write it as "DD + 0 + 0."

Oh, I will just write it as "100." I know that you humans have numbers like 95, 96, 97, 98, 99, 100, 101, 102, etc. Our dog numbers are similar. 0, 1, 2, 3, AP, AP + 1, AP + 2, AP + 3, … 2 times AP + 0, … 3 times AP + 1, … 3 times AP + 3, etc.

Now, Dumb Dog was very patient, but soon he barked, "Hey, I am hungry. I have to go home. It is dinner time." He left, but he had served his purpose. I told him to return the next day.

I know that some of you smart people are saying to yourself, "We discovered how to do this years ago. How else could we have computers that use base 2 numbers, and we counted using base 10 numbers, and we have clocks that use base 12 numbers. The Mayans in Central America used base 20 (ten fingers and ten toes). We use other base number systems also."

I do not care how smart you think you are. Remember, we are just dogs.

I need lots of dogs. I need lots of dogs.

My master said he would be back in twenty-five days. Now I know what he means. It is 121 in dog numbers. Start at the left of the number. The 1 means 1 DD (really 16 in human numbers), the 2 means 2 times ALL PAWS. (Really 8 in human numbers) and the last 1 means just 1.

Let us do the arithmetic. 16 + 8 + 1 = 25. But to me it is 121 days.

1 DD + 2 AP + 1.

Now I can count! Now I can count!

I just need more dogs with more paws. Lots of dogs. Some with one leg in the air, some with two legs in the air, some with three legs in the air. Yes, it works. Every time I try to lift the next leg, I fall. So I just get another dog to represent the next position in the number and start at zero again. I don't need ten fingers. All I need are four "PAWS" and a lot of dogs.

I can sleep tonight. My master will be home in 121 days. I can count! I can count! I can count! Woof. Woof. Woof. I know how many days. I will dream tonight of all the bones that I buried. How many do I have? I think I have 21,313 of them. Where are they?

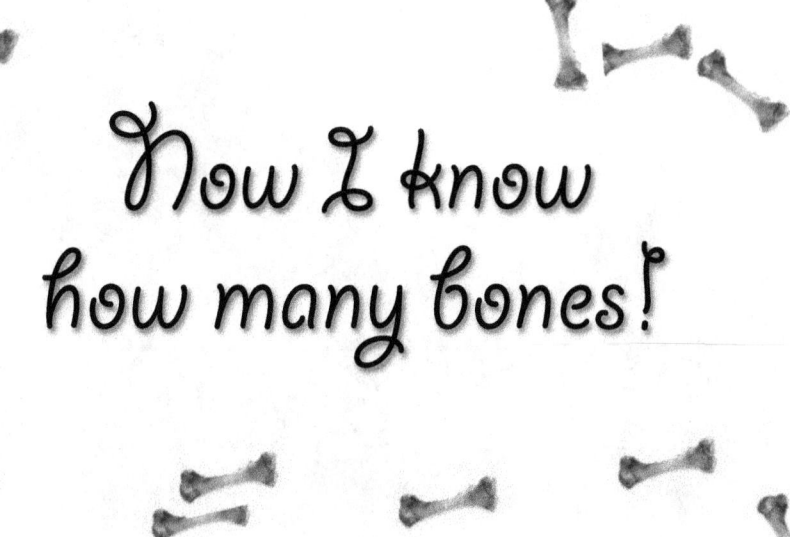

Now I know how many bones!

I will be famous one day! My name is "Snickers"

Famous Dogs of History

There are hundreds of famous dogs. No, maybe there are thousands of famous dogs. No, we are all famous in our own right. There are some special dogs, though, that come to mind as being very special and seem to be remembered more than others. Don't blame me if I did not include your favorite dog. These are the ones my master always talked about.

Rin Tin Tin. That wonderful German Shepherd. He was so intelligent.

Beethoven. He was the biggest St. Bernard I had ever seen.

Laika. He was the first dog into space on the Russian satellite, Sputnik 2.

Millie. She was George H.W. Bush's dog. She became very popular in her own book.

Old Yeller. I don't know who his mama and daddy were. He was just Old Yeller.

Toto. That was the wonderful dog from "The Wizard of Oz." I don't remember ... did he ever get back to Kansas?

The Hound of the Baskervilles. Sir Arthur Doyle. Oh, he was scary.

Wishbone. I love him because he sort of looks like me. Jack Russell. He was certainly intelligent. I guess I am part Beagle, but that just makes me more lovable.

Sandy. He belonged to "Little Orphan Annie." He was the one in the comics who would always go, "Arf."

Nana. She was the dog in "Peter Pan."

Blondi. She was Adolf Hitler's dog. It is a tragic story. It makes me sad.

Daisy. She was always around Blondie and Dagwood. She seemed to be getting into trouble all of the time. Sort of like me, at times.

Lassie. How many of my friends have been named "Lassie"? I like to watch the movie, "Lassie, Come Home."

Feller. Harry Truman owned him. Harry once said, "If you want a friend in the White House, get a dog."

Some of our ancestors even had a price on their head. Patti Page sang that Christmas song: "How much is that doggie in the window?"

Then there were our forebearers who got lost: "Oh, where, oh, where has my little dog gone ... With his ears cut short and his tail cut long ...?"

I could go on and on listing all of the famous names of the past, but I don't have time or space for all of them.

I must name one more. That is **Snoopy** in "Peanuts." Who could forget him?

May all of these, my friends, be happy in their afterlife, wherever that is. I am certain they are still running, playing, making friends, and being just *Dogs*.

I will also be famous one day. My name is SNICKERS. All the dogs of the universe will remember me.

The Mayor's Race

Things have been happening in Dog Town lately that just do not seem right. I have decided that the only way to change the situation is to run for mayor. I am sure that I can win since most all dogs like me, and I can get support from several other animal groups. I can obtain the human vote as well.

"I have been thinking about this for quite a while," says Snickers. "I know what I need to do to win, and I also know how to correct all, well, most, of our problems."

First of all, my platform:

a. We must devise new ways to get rid of groundhogs and raccoons. They continually destroy my family's garden and also the neighbors' gardens. Our owners then get mad at us because we are not doing our job. We do not want to discriminate against other animals, and I know that I am not racist, but those coons with

black circles around their eyes could live elsewhere.

b. Some of the local males have been harassing some of the local females lately. I don't have that desire since I was fixed, but if you bitches will vote for me, I will see what can be done to solve the problem.

c. A wolf killed some sheep recently. One of my best friends, Skippy, was blamed for it. We dogs do not kill sheep. Humans are always stupid, thinking that wolves and dogs do the same things. We must organize a campaign to educate humans of this fact. Local dogs ... stand up for your rights.

d. I propose that all dogs over the age of two be given a dog cell phone. This business of having to go out to the local bush or hydrant to find out what the other dogs are up to is for the birds. I want to sit quietly in my crate and be able to talk with my friends without barking my head off. Cell phones for all! Cell phones for all! Cell phones for all!

e. In days past, our ancestors were allowed to go into stores shopping with our human friends. Now we have to sit outside and wait. I propose that we demand our rights. If seeing-eye dogs (some call them "guide dogs") can go in, then all of us can go into the stores.

f. In certain areas of town, cats are becoming too numerous. There are a couple of large black ones that intimidate small dogs. I suggest that we organize a "pussy." Is that what the old Westerners call it? Let us run these big black cats out of town.

g. Leash laws on all federal and state lands must be eliminated. These lands belong to dogs, all other animals, humans, birds, and the fishes. We are the only ones that are required to be on a leash. Let us organize now and demand our rights.

h. We need to eliminate the term "dog days." This is insulting to us. This is amendment number 1. Vote to eliminate.

i. Stop the abuse of dogs!!! Stop the abuse of all animals!!! If elected, I will immediately appoint my deputy to be in charge of enforcing "Susie's Law." Dogs of the universe, now is the time. Let us unite and stop the abuse of animals.

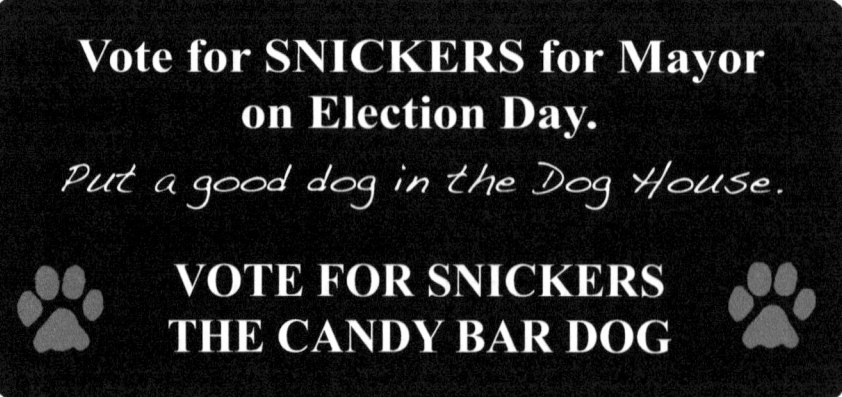

Advice From Dogs To Humans

- Stretch before rising.
- When loved ones come home, always run to greet them.
- Take naps whenever you can.
- Run, romp, and play daily.
- Avoid biting when a simple growl will do.
- On hot days, drink lots of water, lie under a shade tree, and contemplate the future.
- On warm days, stop work, lie on your back in tall grass, and think about the past.
- When you come to visit my master—not for long—remember, I live here. You do not.
- If you do not want hair on your clothes, don't sit on the furniture.
- My master? He likes me better than he likes most people.

Don't let pride prevent us from gaining new knowledge only because it is different.

- Dogs don't get drunk.
- Dogs don't ask for money.
- Dogs don't hang out with drug-using friends.
- Dogs don't eat very much.
- Dogs don't need a lot of clothes.
- Best of all, you can sell their offspring.

Can you do that with your kids?

Sex & Reproduction

It is getting close to 10001. My dreams are becoming more vivid. Am I dreaming? A dog's life is not what it was 10,000 years ago. How about sex? Yea, how about some sex? I must reveal to you now, if you had not already guessed, that I am a male dog. Therefore, what I write in the next few paragraphs may be biased.

Before I go on, I have to make it clear that female dogs do only female things, and male dogs do only male things. There are no such things as females trying to usurp the duties of the males and vice versa. We all know our place, and if we disobey, we will be punished by one of the dog laws.

Yes, but back to sex. That is an important topic to dogs. As we evolved and learned how to communicate with humans, we discovered that adult dogs could have sex for other reasons than for procreation. We had observed adult humans doing "it." Yes, we were watching you, and you didn't know it. We really weren't sleeping in the back room. We also knew that other primates engaged in sex for the fun of it. In our early days, the female just came into, gosh, what did humans call it—estrous, or something like that—every so many days.

Are these mine?

The females would go around exhibiting to all the males in the area, and voilà, they would finally find a male. It didn't take long, since there were always males around at that time of the month. Wham, bam, thank you, ma'am, and it was all over until the puppies came in about 63 days. Then it all started over again.

This never did work too well. We always had too many dogs. We had too many puppies, and we didn't enjoy it. At least, the females didn't enjoy it. We started gaining a little more intelligence, and one of the first laws that we passed, as you have read earlier, was a law to permit mating for life, if desired, and control on all other types of mating. This is by far the best and safest way.

But, as I already stated, why should adult dogs not have carnal pleasures, as humans say, just for the fun of it? The females learned very quickly when they were fertile and when they were not. The rest of the time, hey, let's party. Of course, this still had to be within the confines of all of our laws. Otherwise, we would soon lose a lot of ground in our evolutionary journey to 10001.

I am one of those lucky ones who mated for life. My female is well endowed. We do it whenever we have the urge. How often is that? Do you really think I am going to tell you everything? Let me just say that we dogs could sure teach our *masters* a thing or two.

Bitches: Female Dogs

If I offend anyone in this chapter, I am truly sorry, but understand that I am an Alpha Dog. There are some specific rules that I mention elsewhere in this book, but allow me to exude my wisdom, since I am not only an Alpha Dog, but I am a wise Alpha Dog.

One does not become wise at age two or three, but only after years of experience. This is especially true when it comes to understanding the opposite sex, in this case "Bitches," as female dogs are called. And let me remind you that it was humans who, centuries ago, took a respectful word for our ladies and used it in a most disrespectful way.

Do's and Don'ts: When it comes to sex, we males will do it anytime, any place, with any dog available. Bitches don't think that way. They only want to do it every so many days. I forget how many, but beware, if it is not that time, don't try and hump her. All you will get is a quick bite to some part of your anatomy, and it might be a crucial part of your anatomy. Make friends first, then have a little foreplay if she is willing to participate. You have all day or all night, as the case may be.

More than likely, there will be other males around. That is the nature of male dogs. If they are bigger than you, either visit with your friend later in a secluded spot, or run like heck and let the other males fight over the bitch.

If the act consummates, don't rush it. Enjoy and savor every moment, for tomorrow your master may decide that a trip to the vet is what you need. In the process, you will be changed from an Alpha male. You will become a nice gentle Milky Way rather than a Snickers.

If this happens to be your fate, then you will spend more and more time with female dogs, and you will learn that they are really quite nice after all. You will witness the effects of copulation, the birth of a litter of pups, and you might even have a chance to help raise the little ones. What is past is past, and the future never comes. So enjoy the NOW.

Our God

One of the first topics that we discussed with humans when they finally learned how to communicate with us was the relationship with an Almighty God. They quickly pointed out to us that in the English language used by humans, our name spelled backwards was the same word as god. Well, for sure, that didn't really impress us all that much, since we, along with most animals, have a communication with higher powers, and we have had this communication for many generations. We were very surprised to learn that humans have so many different forms of "religion." We (dogs) just believe in our God. We know that he takes care of "good dogs." There is really nothing more to say. I know that you were expecting an exposé on Baptist dogs, Methodist dogs, Islamic dogs, Hindu dogs, etc. Sorry, but we all just believe in God.

The one that got away.

Dreams

Do dogs dream? Do we dream? Do dogs have fleas? Do chickens cross the road? Do bats fly at night? What do you mean? Do dogs dream?

Some day I will write a book on this very subject. But for now, let us look at some of my dreams and, also, the dreams of some of my friends.

One of my recurring dreams is that I am chasing a rabbit. I am running through the brush and brambles. I am just a few feet from catching it. I speed up, but the rabbit also speeds up. I run faster and faster. Now I am in an open field. I can smell the sweat coming from the beast. It is mixing with my own odors. This is my meal for tonight. He turns. I turn and cut the corner. He jumps over a small creek. I leap as far as I can but land one foot short. Now I must speed up because he is getting away.

He enters some tall grass. Brown and yellow grass is

everywhere. Where is he? He looks like the grass. The grass looks like he does. I am so tired. I slow down and wake with a start. I guess I will eat dog food again tonight. My masters are laughing at me.

They have taken a video of me. I look at it. Yes, I am lying on my side, and my legs are going as fast as they can, just like when I am running. I bet I will catch that darn rabbit the next time I dream of it.

My best male dog friend told me of his dream. He said that, in his dream, he was chasing a squirrel. Why are we always chasing things? The squirrel goes up a tree, but in his dream, he grows long claws like a lion and can climb trees just as well as the squirrel. The squirrel jumps from tree limb to tree limb. He almost nabs him, but the branch is too weak for a dog. It breaks, and he begins to fall. But all is not lost.

He spreads his legs, and they become wings. He gently floats down and does a perfect landing, only to wake up. I witnessed him having this dream one time. He stretched his legs out just like he was flying and then awoke with a start, shook his head a couple of times, and went back to sleep.

My worst dream is when I dream of cars and trucks running over me. I have dreamed this dream several times. I have gotten out of my pen, and I am so happy that I can run and play with no restriction. I don't have a collar. I don't have a leash. I run with total abandonment. I need to cross over this busy road. I forget to look to see if anything is coming. I just want to get to the other side of the road to play. I run as fast as I can. I look up, and there is a huge truck nearly on top of me. I jump, but it is too late. I feel no pain, but I see cars and trucks all over the place with dogs and cats and tigers and whales and elephants and little puppies all mixed together. I try to wake up, but I can't. Please let me wake up. My legs just will not work. Finally, I wake with a start and run over to my master. He holds my head for a little while, and I am okay again.

My most wonderful dream that I dreamed only once is almost too good to be true.

I had spent the entire day leading a group of dogs and humans hiking through the mountains. We arrived home late. I was given something to eat and drink and was placed in my quarters. I was very tired. I had a nice blanket to lie on, and in a few short minutes, I was asleep. Sometime during that peaceful night, this dream came to me.

I was living in a large castle. I was the Alpha Dog. In fact, I was the only male dog in the castle. There were female dogs, pretty female dogs, everywhere. There were other animals in their proper settings, but they all bowed in reverence to me. The tigers and the lions and the cheetahs all lay at my feet. The alligators looked up at me from their moats and smiled at me. The big gorillas came and played

Sometimes
I feel pain just like
humans feel pain.

On a morning like
this morning,
all I feel is
happiness.

with me like I was one of them. The strange but wonderful part was that all of the humans around also revered me. Every piece of food that I had ever longed for was within my reach.

If I had been human, I could drink wine, and I could eat caviar. I had gold and silver in stacks on the floor. What did I need gold for? I had everything I needed. The female dogs came dancing in on their hind legs, each wanting me more than I wanted them. It was an evening to remember.

I awoke. The sun was just coming up in the east. It was so warm. I was very comfortable. Oh, well, there is work to be done. I must find some bones for breakfast. Ah, what a wonderful dream.

Today is my master's day to play tennis. I will be left alone, but that is all right. I will have time to groom myself and reflect upon all the wonderful days and months and years that I have lived. I am getting old. My mind isn't as sharp as it was years ago.

I remember when my master found me. Yes, it was on a tennis court. I have lived a good life. I have given love and happiness to many people. I have been a good dog. I think I will crawl over to my wonderful bed and take a nap. My body hurts, and I just want to sleep. Will I ever see the sun rise again? I am weary. Let me return to my future.

I see this long tunnel with a light at the end of it. I crawl.

I get up. I run. There are all of my friends. Dogs, there are thousands of them. Lions, tigers, and goats are everywhere. Pigs and gorillas and elephants and mice are playing with each other. Every creature that I have ever seen is in sight. They are all happy and friendly and playing and running.

They all love me.

Dreams

It is the year 10001—the year of the dog. We, the dogs, are gaining control. I look at myself. I am young again. All of the other dogs are gathering around to listen to me. I am wise again. They want me to be their leader. They begin to question me.

I am now wise. At the very least, I think that I am wise. As I have aged, I have learned much from my friends and my masters. They have taught me well. I dream and think for hours at a time, now that I am old. If I could only pass my knowledge on to others that come after me. Humans, listen to me. Other animals, listen to me. All creatures, listen to me. I continue to ask myself many questions also. I know not why I was selected to be the leader.

How many questions are you going to ask? How many questions are there to be asked? When I was a little puppy, I thought I was smart and clever. I could perform tricks. I could jump through hoops. I could roll over once, twice, or as many times as I was told to roll over.

Now, now, now, I am old and wise. The young dogs do not understand what I am saying. They do not understand the questions, and they do not understand the answers.

I am the master,
          or am I the slave?

I am the slave,
          or am I the master?

10001 Revisited

What does the word "control" really mean?
Two words:
The "controller."
The "controllee."

Does intelligence have something to do with it? Artificial intelligence? Does the controllee ever become the controller? Is this by design? Is this by accident? Is this by negligence? Is it good? Is it bad?

What does one control? Wealth, time, behavior, food supply, religion, mores, leisure time, mates, laws, life, death, quality of life, afterlife, needs, wants, etc., etc., etc.?

Does your mate control you? Remember, humans have mates, but intelligent machines also have mates, gorillas have mates, dogs have mates, etc.

Does your "master" control you? Remember, your "master" may change. Do you control your "master"? Does your master know that you control him (her) (it)?

The biggest question of all ... Is it better to be the master, or is it better to be the slave?

If I can be the slave and still have everything that I have while I am the master, would that not be wonderful?

The second biggest question is: Do I really know when I am the master? Please remember that the question refers to machines, animals, humans, gods, and all other things in all other universes.

Did man really lose control over the machine, or did he want to become the slave to the machine? It was so nice for man to leave all decisions to the artificially intelligent machine. Now is our chance.

Now, now, now is our chance!

Dogs of the world, wake up. Without man knowing it, we can become their masters.

THE CONTROLLER IS JUST A MACHINE.

Dogs of the world, dogs of the universe, dogs of all universes, unite. Unite now!

The future is ours. The next 10,000 years are ours.

Questions, questions, questions.

Am I dreaming? Yes. No. I do not know.

I am so old. I am so cold.

I hear my master crying in the distance.

THE END

LONG LIVE SNICKERS!

Appendix 1: Counting

DD refers to dumb dog.

ALL PAWS means a dog on his back with all of his paws in the air. It is abbreviated AP.

Some numbers are given in human numbers as well as dog numbers.

Base ten (humans)	Base four (dogs)
1	1
2	2
3	3
4	10
5	11
6	12
7	13
8	20
9	21
10	22
11	23
12	30
13	31
14	32
15	33

Base ten (humans)	Base four (dogs)
16	100
17	101
18	102
19	103
20	110
21	111
22	112
23	113
24	120
25	121
26	etc.

HOW MANY BONES ARE THERE?

21313 (dog) = 631 (humans)

$$2(256) + 1(64) + 3(16) + 1(4) + 3(1) =$$
$$512 + 64 + 48 + 4 + 3 = 631$$

Appendix 2: Rumbagonny Language

Rule 1. If the word begins with a letter A–M, drop the first letter, use the rest of the word + the first letter + A + GONNY.
For example: HELP becomes ELP + H + A + GONNY. That is ELPHAGONNY.

Rule 2. If the word begins with a letter N–Z, drop the first letter, use the rest of the word + the first letter + E + RONNY.
For example: STUPID becomes TUPID + S + E + RONNY. That is TUPIDSERONNY.

Rule 3. If the word is a one-letter word, go to the next letter + the original letter + either A or E as the rules above indicate + GONNY or RONNY.
That is A becomes BAAGONNY. I becomes JIAGONNY. If U were a permitted word, it would become VUERONNY

Rule 4. All grunts are totally phonetic.

www.ingramcontent.com/pod-product-compliance
Lightning Source LLC
Chambersburg PA
CBHW070856050426
42453CB00012B/2226